The Greatest Playground

Poetry by Louis Magoulas

Contents

The Land of Never Never

The Café Lady

Hercules and the Colosseum

The Creator

The Day The Rain Came

Labyrinth of Dreams

A Trip to the Coffee Bar

Candles and Chemicals

Denny

The Greatest Playground

The Lady in the Black Leather

When the Twilight Tolls

WHY

World of Creatures

A Secret Love

The Cave Dwellers – Part 1

A Savage Land

The Town of Terror

The Cave Dwellers – Part 2

The Land of Never Never

Let's hold hands
Forever and ever
It's the time
It's the place
In the land of never never

Let's all wander down
To the beach
That never ends

See the sea serpents
Riding the waves
Feel the magic
Dazzling in your eyes

Cos we are the pink fairies
And we'd always look
After you
In the quietest moments
We'd make you feel blue

The Café Lady

She makes you laugh
She makes you smile
With all that twinkles
In her eyes

The café lady
Mesmerises you
With all her
Flattering suggestions

Her darkened soul
Leaks a forgotten love
And mysteries
That surround her

Yet in the end
She returns to her
Rightful love
And quenches herself
In true happiness

The cafe lady
Prances and twirls
As we believe
She came from
Another world

Hercules and the Colosseum

He walked through the cauldron
Not knowing what fate was awaiting him
The big crowd booed and jeered

And the New Ceasar showed his characteristics
His fowl temperament of his hate for the Christians
As he pointed his thumb downwards

The gladiators entered the rink
Hercules new what he had to do
For this was a taste of survival
Or the taste of death

And as he looked at the crowd
A strange mist appeared before his eyes
It was the Goddess Aphrodite
And she hugged him
And gave him the good news
That in the end he would prevail

And after the skirmish with the Roman Gladiators
He did prevail
For even Ceasar was amused.

The Creator

She was dazzling
Ever so ravishing
A sight for sore eyes

She beamed her eyes
Right over his shoulder
And handed
The canister of water
So he could quench his thirst

Only she could destroy him
As she created him
For he was a man-made machine
Only bent on
Wrecking people's lives

And she came from the planet
Of Alpha Centauri
Where lives are
Ever so drifting
In the dust of the planet

The Day the Rain Came

Well, the rain dropped down
Right out of my hair
I was dancing round
Like Fred Astaire

Where were you
When the rain dropped

Countless yet hundreds
Of droplets of water
Scenic horizons
And countless blue creatures
I guess they came
From the Black Lagoon

Dream of me
And go downtown
Lots of rain
Let's shop around

Well, the rain dropped down
Right out of my hair
I was dancing around
Like Fred Astaire

Hey dude
Don't ignite my cherry
Everybody sings
We're getting merry

Gigantor, gygantor
He's coming to help
Don't run away
We're all in this
Together you know.

Labyrinth of Dreams

Old men bake
Young girls fake
At the height of
The blue horizon

Kings make
To the soldiers return
Of the fine minstrel
In the heights
Of the blind mountain

Where the King of cats
The mighty lion
Runs to the sacred
Labyrinth of beasts

As the lion
Breaks stride
Breathes pestilence
To the mighty soldier
In the labyrinth of dreams

And the sky
Darkens its clouds
Mother nature
Brings out the best
To the cats in the west

Then the bitter cold air
Makes it move to
The children of the future
For their fate is sealed
In the Labyrinth of Dreams

One more Perseus
Who sought the minotaur
Lays in wait
For the monster
Will soon be doomed
In the Labyrinth of Dreams.

A Trip to the Coffee Bar

If the weather is fine
Take your time
And invite the missus
To your friendly café

Don't bring the toddlers
As they will want to be spoilt
With ice-cream all the time

Feel the friendly atmosphere
As the cup of brew is being made
Make new friends
Make a date
You'd be surprised who you'd meet
For love is in the air

Go to the Eureka
Or the Café in Rathdowne Street
Have the Waiter
Come around and say
'Are you being served sir'
I'm Humphries, and I'm free

Spoil yourself, go on
And Mrs Locum will say
'Has anyone seen my underwear'

Candles and Chemicals

Beauty increases
With the streets of diamonds
Alleyways paved in gold
As the master
Shows us the
Enlightened way

The fluorescent lamps
Spell out beauty and decadence
As the master
And the piper
Roll on down
To the awaiting crowd
Who will feel
The final encore
Of the beauty of the caves

For as we speak
Enter the goddess of the
Melancholy shore
That overlooks the entrance of the caves
Only once touched by man

For she will bring luck and good fortune
To those forgotten souls

Then peace will reside
To all those present and accounted for
For this is the land of the meek and the modest

Denny

Denny, a remnant of what was
Survivor of today
Reassured that this will be the new sunrising
And waits for the morrow
Faith, Hope and Charity

The Greatest Playground

In the middle of the newfound land
All the happy people
Have joined hand in hand
As the excitement grows
Still nobody knows

That this is the greatest playground
Where everybody stands
As they go bumper to bumper
In the dodgem cars

As the excitement grows
With all the lucky people
At hand
As the adrenalin flows

Constellations and good vibrations
The night sky gleams
Young boys in excitement mode
As crowds walk out
From drunken bars

Hello to the children
That played all day
In the greatest playground
As Zeus and Hera make way
To the good celebrations

Rythmic sounds
Drown out
From the pools of water
Water nymphs, sea sirens
And good citations Sing belovedly

To all the little children
In the greatest playground
With all the swings
And merry-go-rounds

Sounding as far as the hills
Full of contented sheep
And all the children
Laugh and cry
For this is
The greatest show on Earth
The greatest playground of all

The Lady in the Black Leather

She moves quickly and stealthily
To arrive at her victims abode
She never leaves a trace
She always works alone

The lady in black leather
Takes pride in her work
Although most of her victims
Are men
As she teases them
With her occasional
Greeting card by the door

She has the voice
Of Macavity the Cat
And a soul of the darkest creatures

She leaves a cold flavour
In men's hearts
No surrender
No remorse
Don't look back
She does her worst

She's deadly and darstardly
She makes a mockery
Of those who challenge her

When the Twilight Tolls

When the twilight tolls
Everybody who is segregated
Will be out there
Looking for some action

As the twilight tolls
Animals of all breed
Are running amok
Seagulls flock
As the rain
Passes by
Revealing and disturbedly

As the priest
Reads his sermon
Inadvertently
See the town clock
Transpire into many
Psychedelic transformations

Disturbed children
Blu sky and blurred vision
See the kind-hearted man
Running down track
To come to the town mission

See him enter
And running down
The aisles
Bearing many gifts
To all God's children.

WHY

Why did you
Destroy our City
Ruined the playgrounds
For the children

You lied to your people
Saying that we
Were the dirty enemy
Interfering in your politics

Just think now
You have no friends overseas
Our churches
Our tall buildings
Are in ruins
Our schools are shattered

Mr. President
You made life unbearable
You poisoned us
With your chemical warfare
Just to make your country great
While you are lying back
Cursing and smirking

We have to swallow
Your jest
And your arrogance

So, as the Six Horsemen
On their six white horses
Are on their way
The harlot in purple
Has the last say

A Secret Love

She was transparent
Ever so lovely
Wonderful rhythms of music and drums
Rush through my body
Sending my brain into oblivion

We looked into the bedroom
And saw the searing sun
As I was captivated
By her eyes

She turned over
And said
Drink this potion
It will make you
A prisoner of love

The Cave Dwellers – Part 1

When I think of you
Sweat runs down my head
I really feel misled
I feel like a caveman
Flaunting on his prey
It's the time of day
As the pre-historic monster
Circles around the cave
Is it me, or is it you
I know you
As your eyes are blue
And all is well
For this is the song
Of the Cave Dwellers
And it will hit No. 1
While I'm still around
And the monster is dead.

Savage Land

If you believe in this world
Try and salvage
The forgotten land

Keep your head straight
For all the necessities
That lie in wait

Keep the people blaisee
And the strangers
Would roll down
The infinite
And universal dangers

See the Island of People
Waiting for the illumination
Of the fiery volcano
And all would be swept aside

Silent sleep
Mermaids keep
And isolated hands
Of sea creatures
Scan the turbulent waters
For this is when the pain came
Divers scan the ocean floor
In the islands of the
Segregated population

Town of Terror

There was a loud explosion
As the experiment in the lab went wrong

He came rushing in
He collapsed on the floor
As he spoke out
They're coming for us
Those bone-sucking monsters

We can't escape
We have to do something

I scratched my head
Looking for an answer
We must seek their weakest point
There must be a way

They were coming towards us
Those bone sucking monsters
They were dividing into two
Every six hours

And in the end
After they outnumbered the townfolk
They discovered that water was the only deterrent.

The Cave Dwellers – Part 2

They set their minds
Until their minds blow
With bouquet of flowers
Sent to the wrong address
I'm not fooling
I must confess

Beautiful women zombies
Dance around the square
Maybe it's my mistake
Who knows, I just don't care

But the main phase
It's the prehistoric dinosaur

They search the streets
I just don't care
Maybe they implore
The rules of the Cave Dwellers

And meanwhile the Zombie women
Have reached their destination
Men of all nations
Looking for the degradation
The mindless Zombie women
Have said their final prayers
No more whispers
No one cares

Acknowledgements

Grace Recla for the cover art: gracerecladesign.com and Instagram.com/graszidesign

The staff at Enable Workplace Consulting (Ben Croot, Karen Mace, Hua Pham and Alexina Baldini) for the support and assistance.

IngramSpark for publishing this book and helping a dream become reality.

Other work by Louis Magoulas

The Day The Earth Froze

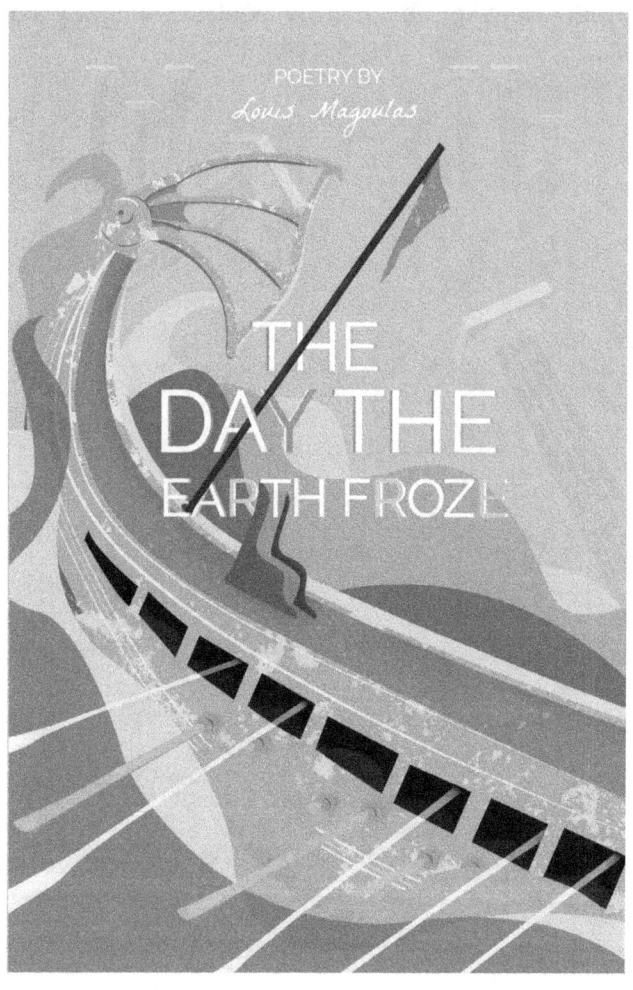